What There Was

What There Was

New Poems

❦

Barry Sheinkopf

FCP

Full Court Press
Englewood Cliffs, New Jersey

Published in the United States of America
by Full Court Press, 601 Palisade Avenue,
Englewood Cliffs, NJ 07632
fullcourtpressnj.com

ISBN 978-1-938812-55-2

*Book design by Barry Sheinkopf for Bookshapers.Com
(www.bookshapers.com)*

Cover art, "Yellow Rose, 1973," by Barry Sheinkopf

Colophon by Liz Sedlack

FOR EUGENIA
Always

PREFACE

Years have sometimes passed for me without new poems. I can't say why. Though it's true, as Auden said, that you're only a poet for a few seconds after you've finished a new one and then have no idea if you'll ever write another, I've had to be pretty patient.

I am therefore grateful for this thin volume. It contains most of the poems I have written since my *Collected Poems* appeared in 2009. I pretty much abandoned punctuation then, and I'm still happy to be rid of it when possible, though I do also try to make my syntax as transparent as possible. (Dr. Johnson rightly warned, "His obscurity, Sir, does not *compel* us to consider him sublime.)

Two sections of this book do require a few words of clarification. The poems in "Privacies" all trace fleeting insights I have had into human nature as I observed people who didn't at the moment realize I was observing them. The poems in "Canonical Hours" follow the prayer cycle of the medieval monasteries; the idea was to capture the essence of each of the three-hour periods into which the monks divided their day, and to celebrate its spiritual meaning. It seemed a worthwhile pursuit for an apostate Jew, and it has kept me out of worse trouble.

—B.S.
West New York, 2015

Table of Contents

GODDESS OF MERCY

(for Susan)

I'm dickering on Powell Street in San Francisco
with a Chinese dealer in antiques
over an early nineteenth-century Quan-yin,
a minor miracle in celadon whose smile
again awakens me. He's had her for at least three years

(I saw her last when I was here back then)
but wants too much for her. I offer him much less.
He squints at me and says, "Okay. I give her to you
for another fifty." "Sold!" I tell him,
having both saved face, and ask to have her mailed.

I leave. Just past the Chinese Gate on Grant
I spot a seated, bearded guy with shaking hands,
in old clothes, huddled up against a wall,
in front of him a empty cup and sign that just says AIDS.
I bend down, slip a five into the cup,

and when his eyes meet mine, say, "Hope it helps."
He nods his thanks. I doubt he sees too many fives.
And when I straighten up and notice,
just across the street (I don't think I'd've
seen it if I hadn't stopped to put the money in his cup),

I spot the one word *Teuscher* on a bright-red storefront sign.
Wow! I think, *my favorite chocolate place:
I didn't even know they had one here.*

I want to buy a box of truffles for my daughter,
whom I've come to care for after minor surgery.

The gal behind the counter's full of cheer—
a jovial redhead selling candy for outlandish sums.
We chat. She asks me where I'm from. I tell her
as I'm fishing out my Amex card—but wait!
The United Airline Visa's. . .*where's the United card?*

My heart leaps. It's the one I used to buy
the Quan-yin. . .shit! I hold a finger up
and call the antique place. But "No," he says, "I haven't
got the card. I give it back to you."
I search my pants, my wallet. There's no card.

I rush out on the street and look. It's not there.
I think of all the hassle it will be
to cancel it and get a new one,
and what if I should need it on the plane back?
Once again I call the dealer. "Look," I say,

"I haven't got that card. I may have dropped it—
could you look outside the shop?" "Ah, sure," he says.
"Juss hold on." Seconds tick. I'm back inside
the chocolate shop. The green-eyed redhead is concerned.
"Hello? Hello?" I finally hear the dealer say.

"I found it lying just outside the alcove there!
You come. I hold. No worry." And I breathe.
I hurry back. The bearded guy's no longer there.
The rain is falling—and I realize Quan-yin
has offered me her first discourse on mercy.

NO WHITENESS LOST

*"and no whiteness (lost) is so white
as the memory of whiteness."*
—William Carlos Williams

What we can't let them know,
of course, is how little
we're actually here—
how the waterfall
at the end of the rocky path
we have been climbing
it seems forever,
the waterfall
that glitters in the sunshine
like a tensed muscle
with all the power
of spring behind it,
does not exist
in this brief world,

(nor the passionate
illicit love we've made
to beautiful women
who understood us perfectly,
the moments we have had with men
whose hands we've shaken
in a felt good-bye
or the glances of mistrust

we've spotted over a bourbon,
men whose characters
we've gauged against our own—
all those whose flesh was never real),

can't let them know
that we have spent so many hours
among the crowd of figments
who flit by us, the whites
of their eyes,
the sheen of their lips
aglow in the shadows,
a crowd more real to us
than living beings,
too many hours,
and that what we have to show for it
in exchange for all that life not lived

are sheets of paper
few will read attentively enough
to feel their pulse
that will never stop beating ever

Look, look again
at the water rushing
over the edge of the falls
like an arm
reaching for the earth
two hundred feet below
glittering in blue sunlight
and tell me
you don't see it

MENTHOL FOREVER

1.

My life like yours
like that of most
is swamped by making ends meet

but a person needs
a little something always
some small pleasure

rarely known by others
Not so much a secret
as a private thing

For me its always been
a shave
I love to shave

Like doing laundry
when you're done with it
there's nothing left to do

I have a very pricey
badger bristle brush
and tub of shaving soap from London

but too often

haven't got the time
to use them

so I also always have
a can of shaving cream at hand
which gets the job done too

though absent
the fine water-warmth
of shaving with a brush

For many years
the firm of Barbasol
produced a menthol shaving cream

I loved
Not you understand
the way I love my wife

but still I felt
a true and faithful love
in what it did for me

when in my ubity
each morning
I would reach for can and razor

2.

Suddenly they stopped
producing menthol shaving cream

I received no letter

to advise my decades-friend was gone
Instead I simply
couldn't find the stuff

on any drugstore shelf
At last resort I called
the company

I spoke to
one of their employees
out in God knows where

Nice woman
Asked her
had they discontinued menthol

Yes she said
it isn't selling anymore
I asked Is any left

in inventory
Yes she said
I said I'll buy a case

It was the last they had
The day those cans showed up
they found a place

in some deep
closet recess

in the hall

and one by one
I used them up
and boy was I distressed

when just a month ago
I started using
the last one

Okay
so you say
big deal

Of course
I understand
I've lost dear friends

this year
seen lives go up
in smoke

seen all those evenings spent
with company and laughter
food and wine evaporate

But my last
Menthol Barbasol
remained a big deal anyhow

I bought that case four books ago
I bought it when my hair

was still a different color

got the photographs to prove it
and what's more
the Menthol Barbasol and I

shared moments
no one else has ever shared with me
Well do I use this last can sparingly

I asked
Decided no hell fuck it
let me spend

this last memento of my brighter years
in recklessness
the way it should be spent

I never thought about it after that
The can would last
as long as it would last

3.

Last week
shopping for something else
in Walgreen's

a blue can caught my eye
I looked and saw
New! Arctic Chill with Menthol!

My mouth fell open
Summabitch! I thought
and bought the first of many cans

Now you may think of God
as Michelangelo conceived Him
burly bearded sort

and you may think
of Him as Her
or It

But only God
say I
could so have timed

that can of Menthol Barbasol
to in a trice renew
my youth my faith

And this
my friend
is not a tiny thing.

< 10 >

EAST BAY INLET, OSTERVILLE, MA

(for Eugenia)

We make our way along a winding path,
part sand, part flattened reeds,
past armies of fiddler crabs
that march in step—
keeping their distance
in such harmony
it seems at first glance
that the earth itself has heaved
beneath our feet—
past stands of shiny rose hips
cherry red
from which tree swallows
suddenly explode
by the hundreds
shooting straight up
throwing slivered shadows
over us, the inlet, all the trees,
almost the sky itself
cluttered with clouds.
They fill the ragged sails
of all that we have lived through.

TANKA II

Halfway through setting
The breakfast table, I see
Two forks, not one. This
Is how your absence hits me:
Out of nowhere, by surprise.

PHYSICS

*(Epithalamion for Elizabeth and David,
September 25, 2010)*

1.

Here's physics lesson one
The distance from the nucleus
of every atom in the universe
to its electrons
is on the order
of ten million times
as great as its diameter
So we are mostly air
are mostly nothing
the luscious feel of skin
the taste of Haut-Médoc
the fragrant scent of peaches
mostly empty space
Physics lesson two
is even weirder
Says that
All of us are moving
right here now this minute
at the speed
of eighteen thousand miles a second
every second
all the time
forever

< 13 >

So as you read this line
we've gone around the Earth
at least once maybe twice
It is a miracle
that in such circumstances
any of us
ever find another
But we do
as you have done
and for this union of the forces
that allows us all to flow through life
as if it were a solid thing
o let us offer gratitude today
and praise of miracles
for you
have wrought
another miracle of love

2.
The ancient Greeks and Romans
offered poems
for a marriage
that were big
on garlands, cows, and running brooks
beneath a mellow robin's-egg-blue sky
It's possible
of course
that they knew something
that we've lost
in all the time that's intervened
They spoke to Socrates
We speak to Facebook

< 14 >

We're more likely now
to see a herd of Holsteins
on an i-Pad screen than in the flesh
But I can still bestow upon you two
the stars and moon and every sun
that ever falls on your enchanted vale
May Tao teach you poise
amid the lunacies
that will beset your years
And faith in sanity the path to joy
And love the way to cherish
everything that's bright
beyond yourselves

ETIENNE MARIE BÉCHET

He lies the stone says
in the inalterable country
of eternal peace—
artillery commander
in the U.S. Revolution
one of the founders
of West Point

The grave is in a corner
of St. Paul's churchyard
in lower Manhattan
just across the street
from where the Towers used to stand
Inalterable irony
to have been so close

< *16* >

THIS EARLY APRIL MOTH

This early April moth
unraveling like string
above the first green leaves
entices me to fling

away my day and walk about
But I have work to do
and no time to be out
drenching my shoes in dew

Privacies

SHE USED TO SAY

She used to say that she requested
things from her husband
for her and the girls

stuff from Bloomie's
Broadway shows
vacation trips

and I'd see the slightest
upward curl of the lip
when she said it

That was the word she used
requested
Didn't *ask*

I guess it must have seemed
more. . .what? Genteel?
She worried about pleasing

had to get it right
to be devoid of fault
It didn't work

He left her anyway
embittered woman
lost

< *21* >

And looking back
these many years
I wonder

would it have mattered
if she'd asked?
It might have changed her

< 22 >

SO MANY PEOPLE THINK

So many people think
it matters
where they live

that if they move
someplace they've dreamed of
they'll escape

whatever chains them now.
You one of them?
I'm not

When I move
worlds I made depart
and others take their place

ONE MAN I MOST ADORE

One man I most adore
in this world
starts to drum his fingers
on his folded arms at times

not because he's bored
but rather that
he feels another's sorrows
so acutely

he has found this way
of letting go
It touches me so much
each time I see it

I could cry
Not that he's found a way
to cope
but that he cares to start with

< 24 >

CONTROL FREAK

Nobody likes
to be in the presence
of a control freak

but I've noticed
there's a spot
on their jaw lines

maybe halfway to their ears
that twitches
ever so slightly

when they're setting out
to drive you nuts
with their quick questions

and their pressing needs
By all means be of help
But look for it

< 25 >

HER EYES ARE FULL

Her eyes are full
of worry
You can see it
where the crow's feet
have begun to form

But she walks
the way she did
when she was
in my college class
so many years ago

She's like a boy
loping off
to a nearby pond
with a fishing pole
bouncing on his shoulder

< 26 >

BETWEEN THE GLANCE
AND GAZE

Between the glance and gaze
men tremble
women turn away

The eye that sees thus
grasps so little
Only the heart

pleads for the fabric to part
uncover yielding flesh
in the peachtime glow

of afternoon
when life wanes
shambling into itself

Only the heart
will ever understand
this fearsome tension

< 27 >

HAVING EMPTIED
YOUR DISHWASHER
(for Howard Pollack)

Having emptied your dishwasher
I see the same three things
I don't know where to put away

a square ceramic dish
a plastic tablespoon measure
and a silicone brush

Everything else
after twenty-five years
I know what to do with

Why this trinity
I'm not quite sure
But it's so a part of you and me

< 28 >

DESPAIR IS NOT A STATE

Despair is not a state of mind
but a thickened coating
on the eye
visible especially
from the side

It always comes
as a surprise to me
to see it
Sometimes people you'd think
will surely have that look
don't
and sometimes those
you couldn't imagine
would have a reason to
do

It must have
something to do
with courage
however it happens
that some people stand
and let what tortures them
go through them
like a blade of pain
while others can't

< 29 >

avoid the blade
that cuts them deep and stays

We are all such slivers of bamboo
driven by the heavy winds of life
that it's a miracle
if any of us
manage to escape
that thickening
as if the eye has grown a nail

THIS THING BETWEEN US
{for Steve Swank)

This thing between us
two straight men
is full of fences
Not the ones
that rule out sex
(I am not so inclined
nor do I think are you)
but those on which
a sign hangs reading
Will He Steal Your Kill?

It is of course
beside the point
that neither of us
hunts for meat
or even
that we grew up knowing
hunger ought to share

The hunting now
is mostly
for who sits before the salt
who rules
who orders
For me instead

what matters
is the look
that passes
when we meet
and grasp again
that we can breathe
as easily as if
the other
were a female

while so many
of our brethren
go on stalking
mastodon
on streets
in offices
big hairy things

So fine for once
to be out on a prairie
where the fences
have been taken down

THE TERROR IN HER

The terror in her
masked itself
as riveted concern for me

But aren't you afraid
she whispered
to be going

Under The Knife
I laughed
I shouldn't have

(the taut skin
all around her eyes
we proof enough)

but otherwise
I might have tripped
into her fear

She took the laughter poorly
No I said
in an even voice

I'm not at all afraid
But but
you *should* be she insisted

Canonical Hours

PRIME

I offer thanks once more
for the morning light
through my bathroom window

as I lather up to shave
It isn't much to think
although I freely pause

to think it
For here
in the ritual space

I enter once a day
where silence turns to song
I still can ask

of all eternity
for one more grace
To love and be loved

and acquaint myself
with oddity and yearning
like a vine

on a less than easy purchase
strained by heavy weight
but reaching upward

< 37 >

in a daily stretch
against the odds
For it is time again

to leave behind
the flavor of it
for the living light

< 38 >

TERCE

However we get here
by now it's happening
each day

kids in their classes
people nursing coffee on the job
light falling in through windows

But as I open mail
write checks
make sure my papers

are in place
I sometimes catch the scent
of a frigid dust on the wind

and bearded creatures crawling
past an upland tree line
hunting with sharpened sticks

for something raw to eat
The image comes and goes
an insubstantial whiff a dream

but there it is
and for the time it takes
I wonder just how far we've come

How much we've eaten
bred, endured
How little we have learned

< 40 >

SEXT

Is it
the absence of shadows
that makes me tough enough

to trust that all is well
in the humid jungle of my heart
and make it through?

To feel the sleepy thud
of sun and torrents falling
from an aimless sky is common enough

for bipeds
who can blush
and reason

but the flatness of the light
plunging to uncertainty
causes a tremor in my eyes

NONES

All men are cowards
in fading light
that slaps long shadows
on the grass

when their vital rhythms slacken
and dishonest hopes
reveal themselves
for what they are

All men are mortal
all but me
the nursery rhymes all say
But here

no angels sing
My hands look old
in such a light
my dreams so out of touch

< 42 >

VESPERS

Off to the right
two ladies guess
how high a hemlock
must have been

the year Bill
left for Yale
(ladies in pink
and blue, whose sins,

if any, never ran
to talking loudly)
and the shade,
like a bell at twilight

spreads around them
hushing the cars
the clapboard white
the river caught in flight

COMPLINE
(for Mae and Dan)

When you were living
and the evenings
bubbled like champagne
I used to wonder

how long there would be
For we exist
on such thin ice
between a nothing and a nothing

suspecting
that even the slightest bit of it
will matter little
up that road to nowhere

Now you're gone
I realize
it always matters
And that what we call illusion

in our innocence
is our reality
spinning atom by atom
to the edges of the universe

< 44 >

as if
we have been writing
all this time
across the surface

of eternity
in ink
that cannot
be erased

LAUDS

I can hear a pin drop
in the fertile dark
as if I've come alive
in stolen time

each creak of settling walls
the cries of far-off cats
the whistle of the freight trains
rumbling five miles off

No one ever knows
what others do at one a.m.
We don't discuss
such things

I shuffle to the living room
wrapped warmly in my terry robe
(for sleep's deserted me)
in search of anything

worth reading
books I've read
a half a dozen times
and gladly will again

sharing the pindrop

WHAT THERE WAS

of my quite small life
with old friends
I have shared it with before

< 47 >

Barry Sheinkopf has been writing poetry, as well as novels and both short- and long-form nonfiction, for over fifty years. He is director of The Writing Center in Englewood Cliffs, New Jersey, where he has taught writing and provided editorial services for nearly four decades. He is, as well, the publisher of Full Court Press, which currently has over 175 titles in print, and he teaches writing as an adjunct professor of English at the College of Staten Island. Mr. Sheinkopf is an Active Member of both the Authors Guild and Mystery Writers of America. He and his wife, Eugenia Koukounas, live in Northern New Jersey.